SEASONS

POEMS FROM THE SOUTHWEST JOURNAL POETRY PROJECT

Edited by Doug Wilhide

TROLLEY CAR PRESS

SEASONS:
Poems from the Southwest Journal Poetry Project.
Copyright © 2010 by Doug Wilhide.

SEASONS:
Poems from the Southwest Journal Poetry Project

ISBN # 978-0-9777915-4-5

PUBLISHED BY
TROLLEY CAR PRESS
3019 West 43rd Street
Minneapolis, MN 55410
612.926.3939
wilhide@skypoint.com

Information about this book, including purchasing
information and quantity discounts, may be obtained from
the publisher at the address above.

All of the poems in this book have been published previously
in the *Southwest Journal*, 1115 Hennepin Avenue South, Minneapolis, MN 55403.
Some of the poems also have been published in other periodicals and books.
All poems are used with the permission of the authors.
All illustrations are used with permission of the artist.

edited by Doug Wilhide
designed by Pamela McFerrin
illustrations by WACSO

printed by Ambassador Press, Minneapolis

First Printing September 2010

6 5 4 3 2 1

This one is for the poets.

FOREWORD

Two things you want from your local poets: quality and quantity.

The southwest corner of Minneapolis is blessed with both, which is why, in 2007, we restored the tradition of publishing poetry in the pages of the *Southwest Journal.* We call these quarterly spreads the Southwest Journal Poetry Project and we have been able to review nearly a thousand very good poems. We also have been lucky to include work by an illustrator who signs his art WACSO, which stands for "walking around checking stuff out."

The book you're holding contains the best of the best of the first three years of the Poetry Project. More than 100 poems are included and more than 40 poets are represented. They are enhanced by a rich sampling of WACSO illustrations.

Putting this book together has been both a challenge and a joy. How do you select from work you've already concluded is worth publishing? How do you not include everything? How do you establish categories in an anthology like this? And just what kind of poetry book IS this?

No one said being an editor is easy, but this time the joys far exceeded the challenges. Re-reading these poems has been both inspiring, and heart breaking, as well as surprising, moving and funny. There is such diversity! Most of us live in and around a small area of a medium-sized city in the Midwest, but our points of view come from all over the place. Maybe this is because Poetry Project poets range in age from 4 (!) to over 80 (!). Maybe it's because people who live here are both deeply attached to the place and widely experienced. Or maybe it's just because we have spent time exploring the infinite territory of the heart.

While there are many voices in this book, some stand out:

Joe Alfano writes what amounts to a daily journal of reflections as he walks around (and sometimes across) beautiful Lake Harriet.

Maria Campo offers a searching engagement with love in its many manifestations: love hoped for, love lost, love enjoyed, love between adults and love for children.

George Scott (G. Scott) is an expert writer of limericks. His offbeat sense of the world captures classic jokes and folk stories in poems that are both funny and thoughtful.

Gayle Mohrbacker has an empathy with her subjects (and her self) that is deeply moving and beautifully expressed.

Howard Osborn weaves word play and an amused sensibility into poems that are as distinctive and entertaining as he is.

My own poems are a series of musings on life, change, seasons, and coming to some kind of acceptance with getting older.

The WACSO illustrations are a perfect fit with the poetry. Their casual, bemused images reflect both superb artistry and a true lightness of being.

Our poetry spreads are seasonal, but the poems themselves often are not. I found that, while summer and winter were well represented, spring and fall were a little light. Maybe the poets are busy with other things in the often brief turning seasons in Minnesota. Or maybe it's just that winters here are long (you may have heard) and summers, for the same reason, are treasured.

Since many of the poems didn't fit into four seasons I had to add categories. Love poetry, as usual the largest group, seemed to cross the lines -- seasons of the heart are not the same as season of the calendar. Poems by and about children seemed to deserve their own category. There was a group of poems that were about (more or less) distinctive characters, and another group whose whimsical approach seemed to define them. The final category, "transitions" includes poems about the changes we experience as we move along life's pathways.

In some cases I tried to establish "conversations" among the poems, where one poem, or a small group of them, seem to be commenting on similar ideas and insights. In this sense the book is a kind of continuing narrative, or at least I thought so at the time.

Whether or not any of this holds up, the poems themselves are what this book is really about. There is no central theme, no guiding feeling or driving purpose, no easy categorization. This is not a collection of Midwest poets, young poets, old poets, male or female poets, funny or profound poets. It's simply a collection of poems that, for one reason or another, deserve our time and attention.

I still cling to the old English major's belief that a good poem is both valuable and enough. I hope your reaction when you read them will be the same as mine: aaah!

Doug Wilhide
Poet Laureate of Linden Hills
Contributing Poetry Editor, The Southwest Journal

ACKNOWLEDGEMENTS

This book, and this whole venture, would not have been possible without the talents of the poets included. My deepest appreciation and gratitude to all who have submitted poems to the *Southwest Journal* Poetry Project, and especially to the poets who have allowed their work to be published here.

No poet is quite comfortable with the old adage that "a picture is worth a thousand words," but the Poetry Project illustrations by WACSO have been a delight from the very beginning. The ones included here complement and compliment the poetry and make this book both a visual and verbal treat.

Sometimes you CAN judge a book by its cover. We are exceedingly fortunate to have the talents and time of designer Pamela McFerrin, who has labored long and diligently to produce a book that looks as good as the work it includes. Thanks also to my wife, Jean, who engaged in the thankless but critical task of proofreading.

The *Southwest Journal* has published poetry in its pages -- off and on -- for 20 years. This is just one of the reasons it is the standout local newspaper in the Twin Cities area. My thanks to the SWJ for its support of both the quarterly poetry spreads and this book. Neither would be possible without the encouragement of editor Sarah McKenzie.

SEASONS:
Poems from the Southwest Journal Poetry Project

SPRING

HALLELUJAH AND TO HELL WITH SPRING CLEANING
Deborah Malmo

Years ago, when I was small and housewifery was all but a sacred calling,
spring came and mothers went—
deep, deep into cleaning.
With an unholy gleam in their eyes, these vernal, maternal exorcists
donned husbands' overworked shirts and set about routing out
the dusty dreams of layabouts like me.
Intent on conversion, fresh air and dispersion
of daydreams and mental malingering,
Mom would fling open the formal drapes in a fit of righteous fervor,
hell-bent on exposing my invisible friends, I guess.

She'd anoint every inscrutable surface with the astringent of her religion,
mixtures of sunlight and vinegar
a dousing atonement of ammonia.
Even the worn rag rugs gave up their dirty secrets
when she performed her public caning.
And when it was over and she was spent,
my rosy, rapturous mother
held her broom on high
and declared herself victorious over
dirt, dust, mold, and must.

I am no such evangelist, but another kind of mother,
not married to my domicile, nor spouse to any house.
Aromatherapy and feng shui can go a long ways these days.
See me spritz the kitchen with scents of sandalwood and heather.
I'll wave my white dust cloth (that miracle of modern microfiber)
in surrender, give in to the siren call of seratonin -- enhancingly,
unseasonably, enchantingly,
wickedly wonderful spring weather.

Life is good, life's a thrill in our condo in Linden Hills,
all the granite and stainless is gleaming.
Hallelujah, and to hell with spring cleaning!
I am keen for the bliss of the season's first cold kiss:
the snow-white curl
on a cone at the Dairy Queen.

WAGGLE DANCE
Howard Arthur Osborn

Let me hear again
   the whisper of the bees.

Let me watch the waggle-dance
   that tells just where and when
to go for that sweet nectar
   held there yet for me.

Let me savor and caress,
   sense again that iridescent
ultra-somethingness
   whose wave-length no one can guess.

Strum for me, and stretch
   the vibrant tension of that moment
till it soars from sweet expectancy
   to ecstasy.

Reprise the entire melody
   subsumed in buried memory
and hum again
   that harmony for two.

LAKE HARRIET, MARCH 7TH
Joe Alfano

On the edge of the ice
etched in sand,
dry rivers with deltas
connect to fingers of
exposed lake,
filled with ducks
that swim in tight circles.
Other ducks
wait their turn.

For now,
the paddling keeps
the water open
and sends small ripples
under the ice.
Have the fish noticed?
Do they wait their turn
to swim in small
circles of sunlight?
Inside my boots
I flex my toes.
It is too soon
to step out
and touch.

LAKE HARRIET, MAY 8
Joe Alfano

In May
the cedars
on the north shore
stand out
with their darker greens
and deeply grooved bark,
gnarled and ready to peel.
Their surfaces
show the knots and scars
of former limbs,
the results of a long life
and the sharp saws
of spring hires.

FIVE HAIKU FROM TAKAYAMA
Doug Wilhide

In Takayama by the river
small feet step quickly.
Spring is late.

The river moves
the mountain's winter
past Takayama's cherry trees.

Cherry trees bloom in the mountains.
The Shogun's floorboards
squeak like small birds.

Icy falls carry cherry petals
tumbling down from Takayama.

Charcoal fires haunt
old houses above Takayama.
Tokyo blooms.

ANTS
Rebecca Surmont

In spring I long for peonies
Their deep crimson stalks
In early May
Erect and absolute
No matter what twists winter played
And the ants marching across the buds
An army
Prying loose each petal
One by one
Peeling
A sun
Spot revealed in the center
The golden prize.
Flowering is fully dependent
On ants
Their life task --
Exposing temporary beauty
I do that too
With you.

SUMMER

LAKE HARRIET, JULY 1
Joe Alfano

Hatched midges come together
to mate in frenzy, zip erratically
hundreds of tiny
punctured balloons
in a cloud
of sneezed aerosol fuzz
that leaves walkers
with grimaced faces
trying to exhale only
while waving arms and body:
dancers at the party.

LAKE HARRIET, JULY 18
Joe Alfano

June bug
a month late,
in a summer
that came early,
is sniffed by dogs
and dodged by feet
as its slow carapace
shoves its way
across the blacktop path.

LAKE HARRIET, AUGUST 7
Joe Alfano

The glassy water
reflects boats moored to its surface,
a strange species of distorted but
symmetrical butterfly

From this mirror rise
fish that break the surface and disappear,
teasing the fishermen on the shore,
who take the bait and cast their lines
toward the sky.

CHIPMUNK
Phil Calvit

I wish my yard,
particularly the deck in back,
to be known among chipmunks
as a place inhospitable
to chipmunks,
a fear zone where there is,
in the harshest, most absolute sense,
no free lunch,
where the smart munk will doubt
an offered peanut (not native here! I mean, hello!?),
lest the trap-door clank down
and you find yourself car-trunked,
bound for an unknown destination
at least five miles away,
released amid fertile woods
in which to make your new home,
but from which you have no hope
              —no hope whatsoever,
even using your vaunted "animal senses" —
of finding your way back to the deck in my backyard,
where my trap, and my cruel peanuts,
await you and any of your friends
who have not yet gotten the word.

SUMMER 1967
Gayle Mohrbacker

Age twenty then, in Berkeley.
Sixty now, in Minneapolis,
where it's warm
in a Berkeley way today.
Mulberry air though
where jasmine would be.

I could be on my way down the hill
to Telegraph Avenue
and Café Mediterraneum.
Walking in the sun with books in my arms
takes me back to that summer
of loving you.

You came out of war into the coffeehouse,
and found me missing Minnesota
in Berkeley.

In your attic room with cantaloupe shells
and photos of your girl back home,
we talked of everything
but love.

Then one day you said,
"Very hard time for mixed children."
You were wrong.
You were right.
It depends.

I had the baby I imagined and then another
whose struggle you foretold.
You would be sixty-six now.
I hear you say, "Imagine."

I imagine us at ninety,
living across the alley from each other
in Minnesota summertime.
From a distance we look alike.

We sit in soft tan pants
and identical plaid shortsleeved shirts,
Our whitegrey heads
together over poetry or our microscope.
You make that sound you always made
just before you laughed.

Now our San Francisco children
make that same sound
on the phone with me over the miles.
Our teeth are in my head
with the college education you made me finish:
"We need a degree between us," you said,
"and I don't have the time."

JACKIE
Paul Walker

Early summer
Sunny Saturday afternoon
I'm sitting on the deck
Trying to find that place where there are no worries.

He is nine years old
Hunched over the pond by the side of the house
He looks up to ask a question
That shows he's figuring out how the world works.

I look into his eyes and see
the beginning of the universe.
As he turns away I catch a glimpse
of the end of the universe.

And for a brief moment I understand
Time...
Infinity...
God.

Please stop growing.
I can't bear the thought
of you leaving
Me alone.

STRANGE CATCH
D.B. Hart

Pooled in the mouth of a country culvert,
three blush and burnt-red koi nibble
a floating willow twig.
Self-arranged, they sway
perpendicular to the stem
like leaves on a bamboo shoot.
Party-colored kites,
these fish fly the far side of noon skies.

Later on, heedless of midnight din --
moth rattle, lizard scream --
a raccoon rinses her hands in the bruised water.
One of the carp flops in the mud beside her,
moon-bleached, palely unpretty.
Tasting it, the coon detects
a hint of sesame,
tang of soy sauce,
burst of ginger.
She chews, she ruminates
over the unfamiliar flavors,
then proffers bits of sushi
to her young.

THE FASTIDIOUS SPIDER
Doug Wilhide

Right after sunrise, as I sit with my coffee
the big spider comes out to inspect her web.
There's a pause while she admires her work.
I take another sip. We yawn and stretch.

Then she gets to work, surprisingly,
rolling the damn thing up!
She's focused and efficient,
hanging upside down,
little feet scurrying like tiny scythes.
The intricate geometry is collapsed quickly;
silk seems to be absorbed into her stomach
and the dew disappears.

She leaves a strand or two attached to a bush
(almost invisible in the early light)
and climbs into the overhanging spruce.
At the end the last strands vanish
and so does the spider.

I put down my coffee and think:
today I must do work this important!
I'll take pictures of flowers before they die,
Give my children advice they won't remember,
Console friends who grieve,
Recollect things no one cares about but me,

Or write poetry.

SHORELINE AUDIENCE
Sandy Burwell

The lake is a satin sheet.
The boat scissors through,
Splits the fabric open and frays it into ripples
Then mends smooth again.

The wake chuckles under the dock
Like Grandpa Duck out to scold the young,
"Get home before dark."
Clouds pull open a curtain
To let the sun set in a pink closing
To the first act.

Now it's quiet enough to hear the crickets
In the tall grasses around the dock.
Cabin doors slam way off down the shore.
A boat putters by, using spotlights;
Drawing a thread-like line on the now black satin.
It glides so slowly that it takes minutes
To pass behind the deck awning
For the end of the second act.

A speedboat roars through the black silence.
"You guys, help me rock that boat."
Laughter at the effort echoes back to shore.
The small boat putters even more slowly in response.

Mosquitoes join the show,
Their place in the food chain temporarily deserted.
Why are the boaters still out?
Maybe the new little actors can't fly that far.
One last cabin door applauds the closing act.

Leaving the theater,
We scheme to acquire real estate
On Boardwalk and Park Place.

A LIGHT RAIN IN SUMMER
Doug Wilhide

I know we looked pathetic in the boat
especially when the rain started.
From the shore we were a small, dark spot
on the flat water, gray as fish scales.

When the rain started, we stayed
As the bigger boats turned for port,
Sailing past us or motoring by.
We stayed and were felt sorry for.

But in the boat we didn't mind:
rain is rain, after all,
and this was just a light rain in summer
and we were together.

We kept quiet. Kept an eye on the wind
Waited for the sun to return to the water.
In the boat, in the rain, on the great gray lake,
We knew no urgent need to head for home.

NEAR STURGIS, SOUTH DAKOTA
Christine Fraser

Coming into Rapid City,
they fly on the highway
like flocks of birds.
Fat, shiny black crows
all leather and chrome
moving steadily forward
gracefully
as one body
in formation
knowing where each other is.
Their elbows spread wide like wings.

Each man rides solo
or with a woman tucked behind him
like a papoose,
her head resting on his shoulder or back.
Hundred of miles flow beneath them
like water in their silence,
only wind filling their ears.

TRANSISTOR RADIO, CIRCA 1975
David Banks

the current connects us, crackling just the same
for the widow nibbling toast at her tiny kitchen table
and the boy pressing hard against the tin

through the pillow for the din of extra-inning baseball
or the song about the songs in which somebody done
somebody wrong

though she has never squinched her face
after tongue-to-tip contact with nine volts,

and he has yet to taste the deeper sour regrets
also housed within that miniature case.

meanwhile, on the eights, men and women of letters
make anagrammatic praise in angelic high harmony
collecting union wage

as a brilliant summer storm electrifies the airwaves —
though lightning, like love, moves faster than the brain.
keep a count for the thunder.

SUMMER'S BRIDGE
Anne Zager

Bitter ends,
Rhubarb stalks and foot bridges
Where bicycles stop
And bare legs step on.

Behold from a wicker love seat,
The warmest night since September:
Spring reclined in summer's hammock,
Men and women loving again
As if in Paris with black coffee
And nothing to do all day.

When you arrive,
We will pick a short story from the latest collection.
I will pay attention for a page or two,
Nod away with hums from the open window,
Drawing a string of drool on your forearm
And my 600 thread count sheets.

Stay, you whisper
Over the fan's hypnotic churn,
As if we weren't already in my own bed.
Still, I will dream I didn't hear.
If you ask,
I was asleep long ago.

AT THE END OF THE DAY
Michael Miller

Echoes of laughter fade over the lake as
quiet returns to the woods and waters.
The last car departs full of tanned sleepy children
and the stuff of vacations at the cabin.

Maggie's trivia question at breakfast was
"Where will you be in ten years?"
We looked at each other in silence
sharing the same thoughts --
so many years already past and
the mystery of how many
may still lie ahead.

But today is today and will last forever.
We talk about the fun, the children,
and, as golden shafts of evening sun
stream through the trees and into the kitchen,
we put on a favorite...
"Could I Have This Dance
For The Rest of My Life?"

We stand silently,
reach out our arms,
and we dance.

SHOOTING STAR
Michael John Kennedy

It slices the layers
in a thick juicy slash
glowing brighter as it enters
blinding retinas in baths
of yellow, blue and purple
before pure whiteout.

Two – three seconds at the most.
completely silent.
letting the light say it all.
not focusing on watching eyes or frozen gasps.

Surprised as everyone else
that the eons ended in cremation
on a moonless Tuesday
at 1:37 in the morning.

BLUEBERRIES
Doug Wilhide

They start creeping north
from about as far south as you can get:
Chili (the country not the soup)
sometime around late February.

March brings fatter and fresher specimens
from Mexico, though the plastic cartons are thin.
I examine closely, turning them upside down
checking for round plump Raphael-like ripeness.

By April Florida has called in, bringing the heat:
waves of fat, farmed, full quarts fill the shelves
so deeply discounted you can't afford not to buy.

We work our way up the coast: North Carolina
ships luscious, juicy, minor works of art. Is that
a hint of mountain moonshine you taste,
or the fresh sea breeze of the coast?

New Jersey blues are part of the blessing
of June: harvested in sandy, coastal barrens,
perfect and plentiful with a salt air tanginess.

Out East the crop goes downeast to Maine
but here in the Midwest we go coastal:
Oregon berries arrive on the shelves
followed by relatives from Washington.

By late summer we are self-sufficient.
Michigan blues are fat and fresh for a several weeks
While Bayfield berries burst with Superior light,
glad to have dodged foraging deer and bears.

You know the end is near when the labels
add a second language and the cartons
come from Canada. The crop is heading north
as the sun heads south.

Winter would be berry-less, but for my secret stash:
the freezer overflows
with baggies full of fast-frozen fruit --
reminders when I need one:
It's always summer somewhere.

MOMENT
Michael John Kennedy

A hot July morning: the sun rising later
as I step out to get the newspaper.
I stand still while breathing the early morning,
Knowing this will pass and autumn will bring
the cold – always faster than I remember --
I pause to hold the heat a moment longer.

Across the street, within your home, you're awake.
Years have passed without even a handshake.
In kitchen light your silhouette makes coffee.
My eyes look down, guilty for what they see.

I go inside, sit, and open the paper.
I read, forgetting you, the warmth, the weather,
lost in the urgency of tabloid lives.
Comics, more known than the color of your eyes.

The street grows brighter, your image fades
Soon winter will come and shorten the days.

FALL

AUTUMN 1947
Gayle Mohrbacker

Mind quick,
judgment terrible.
Wisely though,
he kept short
his visits to Chicago
where he'd have drawn
the wrong kind of attention
and turned up dead.

For all the grief he gave her,
he could've been a trumpet player.
Loved money -
thought saving it was wasting it.
He always knew
when she had something
squirreled away.

Hadn't wanted the baby,
then saw her -
wanted to name her
after his mother.
He imagined her grown up
driving alone in a red convertible.
This would have meant
he'd managed to become rich.

His wife left him a day before
their tenth anniversary.
He was away.
There was no divorce.
She wrapped her wedding rings
in waxed paper with the words
"NOT LOST"
and pushed the little packet down
between streetcar seat cushions
on the way to the train station.

THIS OLD HOUSE
Jim Russell

The cupboards squeal, the floorboards groan,
The stair steps pop and squeak.
The racket is enough to catch
A sneak thief in mid-sneak.

But nowadays such noise annoys,
You're asked to do without it.
You sand and shim and pound and plane
(And glue, while you're about it.)

Then in the silence of the night
Bereft of creaks and squawks,
You realize that all that din
Is how an old house talks.

The message of the creaking hinge,
And all that other clatter,
Is "Come on in, you're home at last."
It's all that really matters.

NAKED FLIGHT
Michael John Kennedy

The birds fly south in flocks by the hundreds.
I stop and watch while dawn is pink and huge.
The river of ducks, grows, flows, and floods.

I wish I could stay; admire this sky fugue.
The sails of wings, the silent understandings.
Like stars – a mystery beyond clues.

My eyes lower to the city traffic.
I watch my step crossing the street.
Above they fly with no sense of panic.
I rush – my shoes clamping around my feet.

WINTER

FOOTPRINTS IN THE SNOW
Michael John Kennedy

Along a city sidewalk they blend together
making their story confusing and enigmatic:

Large boot prints
dog prints
two children
a woman's shoe prints.

The footprints are jumbled,
melting into each other,
scattered.

The children's prints are everywhere
Parent's prints face one another
then move to the edge by the street.
The dogs veer into the snow bank and the street
One pair of the children's prints follows the dogs
Neither returns...
In the yard a snow angel melts into the lawn.

JANUARY
Doug Wilhide

The first snow is for the child in us
whom we never really forget
and to whom we return in the end:
the child who sees through our eyes.

At night the snowflakes look gray
or, in the streetlight, golden.
They still taste the same on the tongue:
Fresh, pure, with a hint of dust at the center.

HOMEBOUND
Deborah Malmo

The sound of new snow,
settled,
fills my ears with a soft, white
buzz.
Footsteps shatter silence as
I make my way home slowly,
keeping time to clamorous
crunch.

The bus was late,
the streets have shrunk,
and my neat, small house
has lost its corners.
It sits on high,
expectant and glowing,
landscaped with tufts of
meringue.

A shadow crosses a frosted window,
a kid whoops
as I open the door.
A swirl of snow lands on my face,
and the warm air rushes to greet me:
scent of roast beef, soap,
and you.

ALLE STELLE NEL CIELO
 TO THE STARS IN THE SKY
Maria Campo

Buona notte alle stelle nel cielo,
  Good night to the stars in the sky,
buona notte alla neve bianca
  goodnight to the white snow,
al coniglio che ora dorme
  to the bunny that now sleeps
ma che domani tornera` sotto l'altalena...
  but tomorrow will be back under the swing-set.

Buona notte ai tuoi occhi stanchi,
  Goodnight to your tired eyes,
al sorriso sul tuo viso,
  to the smile on your face,
alla dolcezza della tua voce
  to the sweetness of your voice,
quando mi hai detto ti voglio bene...
  when you said I love you...

Buona notte all'aria fredda la fuori,
  Goodnight to the cold air outside,
ai sogni che ti aspettano,
  to the dreams that await you,
e nei sogni tuoi scrivo un messaggio,
  and in your dreams I write a message,
un messaggio
  a message
che in un sussurro e con un sorriso ti dice
  that in a whisper and with a smile says
ti voglio bene.
  I love you.
Buona notte angelo mio.
  Goodnight my angel.

LAKE HARRIET, JANUARY 1
Joe Alfano

The ice sheet,
a water drum with a tight skin,
sings the songs of whales –
deep, low tones,
that change
as the wind blows.

Drawn by this music
I step out and walk.
Below my feet
ice is thick and clear.
Half way across, I stop and look.
The ribbon of shoreline
is full of walkers.

I have belonged to this motion
for 20 years.
If the path were straight
I'd be halfway around the world,
but instead
my path is a smaller circle
that once in a while
leads me to the center.

BOOM
Cristopher Anderson

The frozen-over lakes are booming.
They're a Minnesota species.
Walk onto their ice sheet teeth and
suddenly feel the fractured vibration whacks
as they converse in the deep-throated
boom–whine–ping–groan of giants,
chasing quick lines of gooseflesh up my
arms, making me worry if they're still
carnivorous.
It's so fun being afraid!
And right.

FROM THE PORCH,
LOOKING WEST OVER THE LAKE
Michael Miller

Winter…is right there
over the trees across the lead-gray lake.
For days the clouds have been a blanket
protecting us from the season to come, yet
just behind that line of clouds and moving this way
the sky is clear and cold.

A few more hours and that black line
of cloud and icy sky will pass over and
our old friend and enemy will be here again to stay
until the soft winds of March
bring a new birth of warmth and flowers.

The geraniums by the back door, ever optimistic,
still sporting a few buds ready to bloom,
will be shivering and shriveling by supper time.
Soon the firewood must be split and piled
windows checked for leaks and
tender things taken indoors.

It's time to go inside now, to read, to think,
and to wait for the sun to begin again
its long slow journey up the western sky.

WINTER SOLSTICE, MINNESOTA
Ross Plovnick

On the half-lit shortest day of December
you have half a mind to lash back
at the ice storm snapping limbs
like fingers, ignore the driving snow
that's making roads a crash course
in impossible, pack your car for spring
and drive far south enough to bask
outside boot-free

until your spouse appears, waving
complimentary tickets for you to spend
the weekend cross-country skiing
two-hundred miles north of Minneapolis
at some permafrost resort that's selling
timeshares, and your mind repacks the car
with every tool of winter you'll have to have
to make it past your street.

THE SAGA OF THE NORTH POLE EIGHT
Jim Russell

Santa's dysfunctional reindeer
Are causing him problems this year.
They can't pull his sleigh full of goodies.
No more will they spread Christmas cheer.

Dasher got booked as a masher
He hit on poor Cupid last week.
Vixen has chronic arthritis
Her knees are exceedingly weak.

Dancer has hoof-and-mouth hiccups
He hics ninety times every day.
Comet's beginning to vomit
And Prancer is openly gay.

Donner got drunk at a party
And punched out an innocent elf.
Blitzen, thank God, is still healthy
But he can't pull that sleigh by himself.

Now Santa has found the solution
The toys will get through, with some luck.
That noise that you'll hear on the rooftop
Is a gift-laden UPS truck!

A CHRISTMAS PUZZLE
G. Scott

A man had a beautiful girl friend
Who, sometimes, was a bit of a flake.
She'd call him at very odd moments
To solve problems, or fix a mistake.

One Christmas Eve, she gave him a call.
She was worried, there was no doubt.
She just got a jigsaw puzzle
Which she simply could not figure out.

What does the puzzle look like?" he asked.
"The box should give you a clue."
"On the box, there's a great big rooster,
"With a background of red, white and blue."

He said he'd come over to help her,
So she could put it together.
He got into his car, and drove over,
In spite of the blizzard-like weather

When he got to her place, she was panicked;
And said, "We'll never put it together."
He agreed with her, as soon as he saw it;
But he hated going home in that weather.

He said, "Let's have a small Christmas toddy.
"I'll have a Scotch on the rocks.
"We can look at the storm and each other,
"Then put the cornflakes back in the box."

CHRISTMAS TREES
Doug Wilhide

There are tall ones, thin ones, short and round ones
Big ones that fill cathedral spaces
Small ones that sit quietly
on tables by teacups.

All begin in hope and celebration,
their deep forest smell a promise:
silent nights, holy nights, snow falling,
a new year, a new life.

Give them a little to drink
and they become the life of the party
aromatic, fat-needled,
decked out in lights and ornaments.

The kids love them like crazy
They seem mysterious and so much bigger
from the ground, looking up:
What secrets hide inside those dark branches?

Ours this year was an elegant beauty,
slender and well-proportioned,
with blue lights and a gold chain
girdling her neck, waist and bodice.

We kept her well-tended for weeks
until we become too familiar, forgetful.
Her soft, smooth needles began
to fade and fall off.

In the end, she was moved to a snowbank
where she stood bravely,
facing off against winter, homeless,
then hauled away.

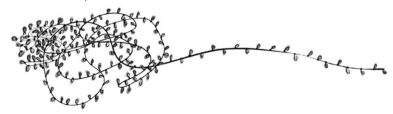

CLEMENTINES AT CHRISTMAS
Doug Wilhide

Wrapped in such beautiful skin,
they withold delight
like a tango dancer tempting a partner.
These are sun-mimes,
silent globes performing in a glass bowl
by a window with snowdrifts outside.

These are Spanish fruit, sensual as summer.
You undress them tenderly, slowly --
thumbs spreading apart their sections
(still lightly clad in intimate undress)
as they spatter droplets into the sunlight.

Half moon, half sun, the clementine
slides into your mouth as easily as a kiss
and explodes into a taste like love
bittersweet, bitter and sweet,
tangy as the ocean air, pleasing as a sea breeze.

This Christmas I am hungry
and want to devour everything:
the sun, the sea, the past, the present,
what I know, what I have forgotten
summer, winter, all of life...

I wonder which is better:
to have loved more than you have been loved,
or to have been loved more than you have loved?
I imagine these Spanish clementines --
small, perfect, summer winter fruits --
Hold the answer but keep the secret.

So in this time of winter dark and longing,
remembering light and lightness,
I choose one, and offer it -- a gift,
a Christmas present for you:
oh my darling, oh my darling,
oh my darling…

MINNESOTA SNOW
Dave Hutchinson

On Monday night, from my warm and cozy chair,
I turned the TV to my favorite weather report.
In Minnesota, winter's no spectator sport.
A blizzard, for the hearty, is like a dare!

Tomorrow's weather: will it be warm and fair?
Or should I head for the south -- a winter resort?
Is there a snow-day ahead? Will the week be cut short?
The answer blows: a Nor'easter's chilly air.

The forecast predicts three feet of snow on the way.
So it's off to the local hardware store I go.
I order a shovel to be here on Saturday.
But three days early flies the beautiful snow

So fluffy and white. It should just blow away.
It's not so soft and light at thirty below!

HOLIDAY SONG
Karyn Milos

Roll out the barrel! Break open the wine!
Rejoicing and singing, now gather to dine.
The hall is made festive with garlands and bows:
Celebrate with us this season of snows!

We wish you good health,
We wish you good cheer,
A good holiday and a happy new year!

The table is laden, the hearth is ablaze;
Waste no regret on the now-bygone days.
Let go of the old year and look to the new!
Feast and make merry and dance the night through!

We wish you good health,
We wish you good cheer,
A good holiday and a happy new year!

LOVE, ALWAYS

LANGUAGE AND ITS HEGEMONY
Ben Shank

No language on earth
so defies literacy
as this rough tongue
of love.

TOWARD MY HEART
Maria Campo

What has a heart to give?

Words flow out of you
words flow out of me
while there is distance between our eyes
there are miles between our hands
there is a wall of voices dividing our voices
there is a wish offered to the wind
for what hasn't yet become you and I
for the story we are not.

What has a heart to do,
when all that it could give
is wasted in the silence that surrounds it?

Find the answer with me
search deeper and further away
look where you haven't looked before
go where your feet have not carried you
toward the point in which I am standing,
toward this heart of mine that is waiting,
waiting for us
to happen.

CHEESE AND CRACKERS
Adam Overland

If the moon is made of Easycheese
then I would like to take you, please,
upon this salty spaceship snack.

We'll surf the wavy worm of cheese away in space
and crash our Saltine satellite
upon that mushy paradise
and out of our little Kraft we'll get,
our moonboots getting stuck in stick
and laugh and laugh
'till easy cheese, like play-doh squished from a machine,
comes shooting out our noses, see,
and other pleasant orifices, wee!

Our lives will be for nibbling then,
I'll nibble your nose and you nibble my chin,
And when we tire of the moon,
although it not be even noon,
We'll board our ship and sail again:
I've heard that Mars is all Wheat Thin.

MATCHSTICK LIVES
Tanja Birke

I know you in the world of illusion,
where we wear our paper crowns
and talk of small truths
like clouds and wedding rings.

In our uniforms of civility,
boxed-up emotions on the thrift store shelf,
we don't dare to strike against the rough,
and our matchstick lives march by
unflamed.

Meet me in the real world,
the sacred circle,
that messy place,
where our hearts make a music
that our feet cannot resist
and we carry our uniforms of civility
in knapsacks,
waiting for the ride back home.

SEEN
Gayle Mohrbacker

It is a struggling store –
You think twice about going in,
About getting their hopes up
When you doubt you'll buy.

There in the window,
A red glass dish, flame-shaped,
Rests restlessly,
Flickering on Lyndale.

Its aggressive gleam chills me
As I walk past in the early evening.
Suddenly I'm speculating
About that girl who carried death
Into the crowded Haifa restaurant.

Dangerous girl, large-eyed
In a deep blue scarf perhaps,
And lipstick for the first
And only time in her life.

Her jacket in the warm evening
Alarms the young military policeman.
But his seasoned superior signals:
No, she's alright.

Lipstick and nervousness
Mean what they always do:
She sees her future
With a boy who's here tonight.

POSTMODERNISM
Doug Wilhide

The first romance I can remember
was that Howdy Doody hottie,
Princess Summerfallwinterspring.
Oh those braids and bangs!
That swaying buckskin!
What was a boy to do?
Dulled by the long school day, too young to fantasize,
I dropped into the fantasy played out before me.

Those after school afternoons in front
of a black and white TV are precious still --
the indecipherable mysteries:
was she all her seasons, all at once,
or something like Summerfall Winter Spring?
Was she related to Wintergreen, the chewing gum?
Were she and Howdy just best friends
or had a threshold been crossed
that could be crossed again?

I learned recently that Ms. Winterspring
(or, actually, the actress who played her)
died tragically young in a car accident.
How sad! Was Buffalo Bob crushed?
Did Clarabel weep? I never noticed a difference,
having moved on to the adolescent delights
of Annette, Darlene and other Mouseketeers
in their stretched sweaters.

In a much-changed world
the original puppets -- I understand --
are worth millions and displayed in museums.
Now it's the memory of beauty
that keeps pulling the strings.

TRUE LOVE
Howard Arthur Osborn

If temptation can be chastely stated
and unbridled lust be bridled and abated
if joy drift with fragrance on a breeze
and love's essence more than tease

then Love I do not misperceive
but in truth your charm & grace receive.
And if my mind, unbounded and elated
to share such love, however much belated,

find that my head with heart agrees
and both with you now feel at ease
what more could heaven or earth conceive--
this is true love not make believe!

  If this be false and on me proved
  I'll try again—I might improve.

SONNET CVIX
William Shakespeare

Let me not to the marriage of true minds
Admit impediments. Love is not love
Which alters when it alteration finds,
Or bends with the remover to remove:

O no! it is an ever-fixed mark
That looks on tempests and is never shaken;
It is the star to every wandering bark,
Whose worth's unknown, although his height be taken.

Love's not Time's fool, though rosy lips and cheeks
Within his bending sickle's compass come:
Love alters not with his brief hours and weeks,
But bears it out even to the edge of doom.

  If this be error and upon me proved,
  I never writ, nor no man ever loved.

BREAK UP
Gayle Mohrbacker

For a year
I lay under the cat and
Buttered all my food.

Then rhythm
A new pulse grew
By itself with time and quiet.

I took three busses
In two directions
To go to the opera at night
By myself.

GOODTIME GUITAR
Shannon King

I want to play the blues,
but you want to play -- Mozart.
What is this disconnect
between my achey-brakey heart,
and fingers plucking furiously
a jazzed up minuet, brighter
than a banjo playing bluegrass?
If you don't stop,
I'll replace you with a harpsichord.

Ah, that Mozart knew what he was doing;
forget those moaning blues
Snap your fingers, click your heels,
Leave broken hearts unspoken.

MOVING DAY (OPUS #4)
Carole Maria Ostlund

    The space between us was only a river
on the day that I moved across it.
From dawn past dusk
you telephoned in phases
consistent as the moon.
Your turbulence met my calm,
though you hadn't given me boxes
or helped me fill them.
On the 7th try you beseeched me
and collapsed in my bed
until your strength waxed
and your guilt waned.

    The space between us became a gulf
on the night past the day
that I forged the Mississippi.
You fled down the stairs in the dark--
you became someone else
when I crossed the bridge
with my unguarded heart
as I traversed the unspoken
muddy, Maginot line.

THAT NIGHT AT THE DANCE HALL
UNDER THE OAKS NEXT TO THE RIVER
Cristopher Anderson

It had been a while since I'd really seen my wife –
until she danced with the other man at the folk dance.
His hand moving along her waist. Her splendid
legs and smile. The arch of her body inside his arm.
When the Swedish dance, the people are one river
swirling and eddying. And women fly, held by men.

This man looks seasoned in the boat, deft hand
on tiller and closely tuned to wind and sail.
Oh, I also dance with her – all elbows and knees
of me brought to the dancing floor.

At the end of the evening, he comes to sit
next to her, talking to her earnestly with eyes misted.
My schoolteacher wife with sunny face and trusting heart –
any schoolboy would tell her everything.
His knee is bent, shoulders square, head tilted forward.
She sits with her back regal, chin tucked in.
Isn't this the moment in the historical novels when
pistols are being readied? Aphrodite loves Ares.

I kneel down next to my wife, but the man doesn't see me.
So much is in his face – just whom or what does he see?
I wait and watch as he talks himself out, my wife including me
with a nod and hand as I try to edge closer toward them.

After, I walk back to the car with the woman of wheat and corn and
raspberries and swimming stars – a blade in her dancing dress.
I overplay the clutch and stall the engine,
get it started again and gun the car toward home.

THE BODY POLITIC
Cathy Cato

The chameleon does not turn color
to match his background like I thought...
Transformations occur to adjust
for light and temperature.
Just as humans wear white
in the sun drenched summer –
this reptile does the same with skin.

Emotions change skin tones too, not
unlike we who flush and blush –
reds and yellows are more visible
when threatened. Anger darkens skin

And when
the chameleon goes a courting
he wears his brightest colors - turns
from brown to bright blue or green
to brilliant turquoise.

The female
says yes or no in colored response.
The rejected suitor fades back to normal,
but at least he knows
there is no
in between.

ALPHABETICAL DISORDER
Karen Barstad

Today I am the letter Q
Round bottomed, unstable
Teetering precariously on one stumpy leg

K and C can do the job today
They'll suffice
While I
Uncertain, superfluous, an afterthought
Shyly disappear into the background

Today I am the letter Q
Incomplete
Without U

SHOULD THINGS CHANGE
Maria Campo

If the seed we planted
should ever sprout leaves,
Write me.

When all the chapters
have been read
and the book has been closed,
Remember me.

When all the options
have been explored
but the only one left
is to move on,
Talk to me.

Perhaps tomorrow
you'll change your life
perhaps tomorrow
I will still be alone.
No promises can be made
but should you change address
and find yourself alone...
Call me.

GOODBYE THEN
Doug Wilhide

We said goodbye then
With people there
So it wouldn't be quite so hard.
And we had said what we wanted to say
Or at least we knew by then
What didn't need to be said,
So it wasn't so hard.

We would see each other again
Though we didn't know when
And we could call and talk
Across the thousands of miles between us.
After all we had known each other
All this time
And would know each other
always and anywhere.
So it wasn't so hard.

But – both of us – our eyes were tears
And the world and the people were not there,
And that last hug –
How could I not hold you?
How could we separate our hearts
When we felt them beating together?
And how – God, how – could I let go?

FRIENDS
Maria Campo

We lean against each other
youth in our pockets
no worries but to finish
a day of playing in the sun

I feel the breath of time
running alongside
chasing a soccer ball in dusty roads
laughing with us at the stumbles
and the goals.

Our shadows now resting in the shade
sweat rolling,
salty drops licked from upper lips,
hair sticking on forehead,
smiles lingering in our eyes.

Your arm over my shoulder
we look at the street
bathed in mellow sun.
Another ending day
slowly slides away,
but with you on my side,
I am not afraid of time.

WISHES
Amber Lampron

A haircut
a fifty-acre farm
a titanium spine
a hairless furry flying dog
a touch of your beard in bed
But not necessarily in that order

A LOVE, A MEMORY
Maria Campo

I can't remember the last time
we loved each other.
It just occurred to me while making coffee.

I remembered some of us
while, with the palms of my hands,
I caressed the wool rug
that saw us embraced.

I can't remember the day!
I remember well the first time,
but not the last...

So soon... you are going so soon...
Taking along the words you spoke to me,
the voice I loved...
What's worst?
The ending of a love or the end of a memory?

I close my eyes and see your face.
I know it by heart, but I can't,
I can't remember
when we made love last...

DANGLING PARTICIPLE
Diana Lundell

A verb is considered dangling when it
doesn't agree with the subject of the sentence.

We don't say,
Flying with love, the marriage is blessed.
We say,
Flying with love, we're blessed with a happy marriage.
And you fell for me because I have all
the characteristics of a good wife and participle:
present, active and imperfect.

We don't say,
Buoyed by good communication, they fulfilled each other.
But naturally, there will be days when our stars won't
properly align, and words said, later regretted.

We don't say,
Cleaning out the marriage closets, many cobwebs were found.
We say,
Cleaning out the marriage closets, we found no cobwebs.
But there will be times we'll keep things from each other
because they hurt, or because we're still trying to work out
their meaning. And days when we'll keep private a concern
to think on it for awhile, but only awhile.

We don't say,
Tired of the politics of marriage, a resignation was turned in.
We say,
Impressed, they offered each other scholarships for 10 more years.
Marriage is like a sentence —
each grammatical element needs to make
sense together to form
a complete meaning—like roots, like bones,
bound so deep that one no longer knows whose is whose.
Missing you would be like losing myself.

DUOLOGUE
Robert Guard

I saw shoes taking a stand for each other
foot soldiers without a war

Two grey doves on a wire waiting for
a pair of shotgun lovers

Dragonflies joined like skydivers in the air
ignoring love's gravity

I knew a woman with one breast
smaller than the other

We were not a perfect pair, but she was happy
and so was I

Lovers lay side by side in graveyards
sleeping alone all over again

Two stones skip like kids across the water
one drops like a stone

The land of left socks has a king, but the queen
has not been found.

MILE MARKER 19
Sandra Nelson

As strains of Wagner weep from the dashboard,
your eyes hypnotize me in the rearview mirror
like two young boys licking their lips
over a sexual fantasy.

Hunkered down in the back seat,
I hug the musty blanket we shared last night
as your rage gnaws at my throat
like a bitter aspirin refusing to go down.

Barely breaking the rhythm of the road,
the wheels suddenly bite gravel, then lift off.
Tumbling airborne in slow motion,
the air between us is finally clear.

Will one of us survive to blame the six-point buck?

CC ME ON ALL YOUR EMAILS
Sam Wilhide

It is important to be personable,
and hard-working, relaxed and confident,
intelligent and dedicated,
to be passionate and to use best practices,
and to first of all do no harm.

It is better to love your job
than to be a workaholic,
because how can you be addicted
to something you love?

I drink-in every moment of your body,
and then I fling myself again
at the ghost that turns its back.

I WANT NO LESS AND WISH NO MORE
Maria Campo

I wish I had more time
To spend together
To do the things we don't do more of
Like laying on the bed, reading our heads off
Or baking together chocolate chip cookies.

I wish I had less to worry about
To keep me awake at night
Pushing me to work, work and work.
I wish I had more energy
To play with you as we used to do
And laugh and do dress up
Or go for a walk.

I wish I had more money
So I would not be concerned about the future,
So I could leave my work for a few hours
And together go see a movie.

I wish I had less stress and could smile more
And be silly with you
Paint our fingernails different colors,
Lean against each other and tell stories
Listen to your heart open up to mine.
Here tonight I wish to be
More of the mom I am in my heart.

But time moves past us
And you are now a young girl
Ready, soon, to let go of my hand
And walk on your own.

I wish I had more time
With the little girl in you, my love,
But tonight I have just enough time to tell you
That no matter what life may bring
The best has already arrived
 With your eyes and the love I carry inside.

I want no less and I wish no more
Than your love.

THE KIDS ARE OK

HAPPINESS
Maria Campo

is looking into your eyes
and in them read love.
To have your smiles
printed in my heart,

to receive
your hand-made cards,
to see you
buy me an orchid
with your allowance

and know,
that even though
it is all you have,
you want to spend it
on me.

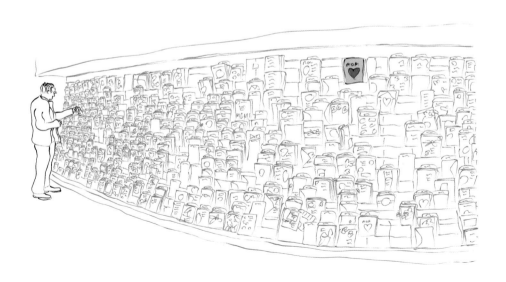

GRACIE'S CONCERT
Jacquie Trudeau

I'm a little startled when I see her.
I often am.
I expect her to be younger, rounder, smaller.

This time when she sees us
She doesn't come running
Just gives us a little wave from her seat.

She wears black and pink glasses now
Which do nothing to detract
From her perfect face.

She walks on stage. Tall, slender
Dressed in black, long green scarf
Her curly hair restrained.

She takes her seat, sits straight
Her clarinet in the proper position
Across her lap.

Once she's on stage
She no longer searches
For our faces.

She plays her piece, focused
With strong measured breaths
While I hold mine.

THE ADVENTURER
Barbara Tuttle

Framed in my window: the monochrome park
and Lake Calhoun with frozen waves.
I've been on ice these months.
The phone rings. My daughter's voice
from Down Under. So clear,
that she and the honking taxis,
the humming crowds of Melbourne
could be across the street. I reel her in
on the filament of voice
I see blue and green, aqua and golden,
An Australian beach.

Twenty years ago
She swam in my womb, my daughter Kate,
her curly eyebrows already knit.
What a swimmer she was even then.
The nurse could not grab a heartbeat
before she'd swim to the other side of my belly,
over and over,
out of reach.

"Stella," we called her – a star in the dark.
As a toddler, before bed in summer,
she'd signal the time for an evening walk
By standing, arms outstretched,
turning in a circle, saying, "Mooooon." At five,
she rode the gyroscope at a local fair
Spinning, upside down, fearless, eyes sparkling.

Now she has flown across the globe to the other side
of seasons and stars, sees the wedge-tailed eagle
and platypi, the Southern Cross in the summer sky.

Here above, the Canada geese
stream past my window through northern air
and I hold her under my heart.

DRAGON DREAMS
Owen Lazur

When a dragon dreams
he sees a castle celebrating
the festival of the peacock.
When a dragon dreams
the castle is totally unguarded,
open for attack.

When a dragon dreams
his flame burns a meal
just the right amount,
crispy on the outside,
soft on the inside.
There is no knight to spear
him through the neck.

When a dragon dreams
His cave is surrounded by small villages
ready to be burned.
But when he wakes up
it's all the same,
large palaces heavily guarded
by knights ready for any attack.

But come night,
when a dragon dreams…

JUSTICE
G. Scott

A young girl was out in her back yard,
Digging a rather large pit.
The neighbor lady leaned over the fence,
And asked the reason for it.

"I'm burying my goldfish," the girl explained.
"It died early this morning."
The woman said, "It's a terrible shame
"That your fish should die without warning."

"But why are you digging such a large hole?
"No goldfish is as large as that."
The girl replied, "I need a big hole.
"My fish died inside of your cat."

THE MORAL
G. Scott

The fifth grade teacher gave out an assignment:
Each student must have, by the next session,
A story that had, in its context,
A moral or life-changing lesson.
When the next class got together,
She asked Billy what he had to relate.
"It's a story my Dad told me one day.
It's about his young sister, Aunt Kate."

Aunt Kate was a jet fighter pilot
When she served her time in Iraq.
On one of her scheduled missions,
Her flight came under attack.
Her plane got shot down in the battle.
As she jumped from her plane, she took stock:
She felt for what she had with her:
Some whisky, her knife, and her Glock.

Beneath her, she saw twenty soldiers
With Iraqi uniforms on.
To fortify herself for the landing,
She drank the whisky 'til it was gone.
Descending, she shot fifteen soldiers,
And knifed four more when she landed.
Her survival knife broke in the fourth one,
So she strangled the last one bare-handed.

"What's the moral of this story?" asked the teacher.
And wondered what the boy's father was thinking.
The boy said his dad learned this lesson:
'Don't mess with Aunt Kate when she's drinking.'"

BOWSER
Cathy Cato

Sometimes when his hands
hold me tight and he breathes
like someone else – my fur
gets wet from his face. I sit
patiently as he caresses my ears;
one he calls nubby the other,
soft. Although if you asked him
he would say the soft one
is the result of rubbing nubby
to smooth.

He doesn't seem to mind
I've lost my nose several times.
The button is fine and I can't
smell anyway.

A lot has changed – I used
to be bigger with longer
tail – shrunk to one third my size.
There are places where my tan
and white fur is threadbare
I was taken everywhere
as a talisman
as a friend.

And then –
I stopped going places.
Spent more time in his room
with Goodnight Moon.
It's a comfortable secure life, he
smiles for me each night
when he goes to bed.

And sometimes –
He picks me up with gentle giant hands
who hold me throughout the night.

FOR MICHAEL
Cathy Cato

My mind was already at work on the way there.
And then, I trailed a school bus.
I turned off the radio
and defrosted the car window.
With each stop I breathed deeply,
and listened to the scenes.

At most stops, there were small groups of mothers
with babies and toddlers on their hips.
Their children, bundled and booted to ward off
the chilling bone cold. A loyal dog
here and there.

In one slanted driveway, a small girl and smaller boy
clad in quilted jackets made their way stiffly,
taking baby steps on a sheet of glare ice.
Tiny feet work only so well; they both fell,
and got up in unison. Falling when one is their size
bears so little danger, especially when padded.
Yet still, there was no one there.

At one stop, the mothers stood in a circle, talking
with each other animatedly,
as if they were all stars in their own movies.
To the side there was one father,
watching all the children
while speaking to his own.
The bus pulled up to an especially icy spot.
The father placed himself between the curb
and the bus – offering a steady hand
to each child. A safe bridge from here

to there.
And, when the bus began to pull
away, the father held his gaze
as he walked alongside,
at the same speed
that his daughter would walk
years from now
down the aisle.

$100 BEAR
Diana Lundell

i. Dad takes me, just me, to the State Fair,
    asks twice if I'm hungry.
    Because I'm afraid to give the wrong answer,
    the first time I say, I don't know.
    He says, what do you mean you don't know?
    you're either hungry or not.
    I should say, you can be in-between,
    but I know the value of staying silent,
    and wait for the swat that doesn't come.
    The second time he asks, I say, no,
    because he's a mystery to me
    and I'm afraid of costing him good money.

ii. What in the hell's wrong with you?
     he says, because I'm dancing in my pants.
     I've waited too long to tell him
     that I have to go to the bathroom,
     and I know I've gotten it wrong again
     when he asks, why didn't you tell me earlier?
     I am a mystery to him.

iii. When he admits he's hungry,
     it'll be safe to admit I am, I tell myself.
     At the corn dog stand he finally gives in
     and asks if I want one too. I just nod,
     which of course is a perfect answer
     that I don't have to speak.

iv. In the Midway Dad uses up his money,
     trying to win me the biggest prize:
     a stuffed, brown teddy bear
     with shiny plastic eyes and a stitched nose.
     I was a goddammed marksman in the army,
     I ought to be able to, he kept saying.
     And at the Battle of the Bulge, he'd sure
     killed his share of Krauts. I don't tell him
     I'm too old for stuffed animals.
     I don't tell him anything.

v.   Without my knowledge, later that day,
    because he feels he's disappointed me,
    he pays Tommy Phillips, the boy next door
    who has a proven knack
    for triumphing at Midway games,
    a hundred dollars to go and win me that bear.
    But even Tommy can't do it, and instead,
    brings over the medium sized one
    with the crappy vinyl eyes
    and the already fraying pink ribbon.

vi. Before bed, Dad calls me downstairs,
    and looking sheepish, he presents
    me with the cheaply made bear.
    Whatever he expects from me, I don't do it.
    Too afraid of saying the wrong thing,
    I say nothing more than thank you.
    Later, Mother tells me the price he paid for it,
    and because I'm embarrassed for him,
    I put the bear away, where not long afterwards,
    it disappears into the land of lost and neglected toys,
    never to be found again. Sometimes things choose
    you perfectly, and you still get it wrong.

TINY HEARTS
Amber Lampron

Your heart doesn't belong to you
Once you have children
It gets torn out
On a regular basis
More often after a divorce.

Every time he pulls out of the driveway
With them in the back
Every time they say
We wish we were always together
Every time you go to bed
And their beds are empty

You think it will be better next year.
But time does not make it better
No breathing to check
No late night coughs
Or extra water in the night
No sleepy feet, faces, warm hugs
To keep the heart at peace.

We think we do all of it for them
Nurturing, teaching, cooking --
Until they are gone
And we realize how much
Is for ourselves.

WHIMSIES

A BUDDHA DAY
Chuck Boe

A fat Buddha smiled at me the other day.
Walking along, minding my own business,
and there he was:
Bald, and huge, with his robes open
and his pillowy chest
and globular belly hanging out,
smiling at me.

Taken aback,
I wondered why he was smiling.
What did he know?
I have nothing to hide.
Maybe he is just being kind.
I resisted the urge to reach out
and rub his belly for good luck.

I wanted to study this fat Buddha,
but averted my eyes.
I'm far too reserved to get involved.
I peeked back at the fat Buddha
as I hurried along.

I wonder what would have happened
if I had rubbed his belly.

STATUE
Phil Calvit

It is a famous sculpture,
surely you have seen it;
a man stands oddly erect
at the bottom of the basement stairs
as if drawn up suddenly by a string,
brow scrunched, eyes narrowed, wondering
What'd I come down here for?

MY ADVANTAGE OVER THE MOON
Phil Calvit

My advantage over the moon is that
every month or so, as he remakes his face,
at the completion of my haircut
a young woman lays down her shears,
picks up a black-lacquer-handled mirror,
and I get to see the back of my head.

RANSOM
Kevin Zepper

...now listen closely, listen good.
I've kidnapped your poem
and if you don't do what you're told,
you won't see your poem again–ever!
I'm not going to hang on this cell long,
so don't pull anything tricky.

Sounds like you got the little present I sent you.
Yeah, I cut a line off your precious poem
to prove I mean business.
Yeah, yeah, call me what you want
but I've got your little verse tucked away
and I'm calling the shots.

Here are my demands:
I want a complete, unabridged set
of the Oxford English Dictionary, the index, too.
No CD-ROM crap either. The real deal.
Meet me behind the Noble Barn at midnight.
Go to the second dumpster where they ditch
the tear covers and romance returns.
Stuff the OED in a big green lawn bag, two-ply,
and put it on top of the dumpster lid.
I'll set the poem in its place
after I know no one's followed me.

Let me be clear on this,
if you've dragged the English Department in on this
I'll have to cut your poem a little more
and a little more and a little more...

Be a smart poet and don't try anything heroic.
I have a degree in American Lit
and I'm not afraid to use it.
Remember; no funny business...

HOW THE POLL IS CONDUCTED
David Banks

We'd like to know, or not know,
what you think, or don't think,
depending on whom you are

or whom you feel you might be.
Your opinions matter
to those who will agree,
or not, with our findings.

We prize diversity.
We believe in this so strongly
we will erase you from our results

if someone just like you
answers first, and answers freely.

Do you believe in numbers? We snare
a margin of 3 percent
90 percent of the time.
How 'bout them numbers?

We've been around for 50 years.
We've had multiple partners.
(We've always used protection.)

Please pick up.

CONTENTMENT
Cathy Cato

Curled like question marks
on the satin brocade cushions…

The black and white one
raises one forepaw to shield the light,
the other is tucked under his warm fur,
lightly covering a hint of pink skinned belly.

The other, with a coat of black spots
on a ruddy background sleeps languidly
with her tail coiled around her slim body.

Once - when I snuck into the room
well after dark and laid an open palm
on each belly, they didn't stir –

but their purrings rose
as if my hands had turned up
the volume.

EEK SQUAD
Howard Arthur Osborn

They say there's more than one way
to skin a cat—
or be skinned--at that
so anytime you feel you're being flayed
for your views or tattoos, come to
SEMIOTIC TRANSFER SERVICE.

Change your mottos, your lover's names
or games, even your priorities.
Try puzzle teases. Join the dots.
Sudoku and the Wheel of Fortune.
Clue and treasure hunts.
Invent your own game. Just try it once.

Fifty percent off on good news days!
Divorces are our specialty—get two for one!
Bring your next of skin (new or old).
Have old tattoos mounted in a video scrapbook
(no pornographic shots allowed).

Where do you draw the line—or did you draw the line?
It's art! Get smart! TATTOO BACK GUARANTEE:
If she or he comes back, get your tattoo back
(embellishments extra).

Ask about our secret service connection:
avoid parental discretion, use your own.
Cover-ups? No questions asked.
Yes there is a cover charge—not large,
just one percent of your after tax income.

Latest technology brought to you by the eek squad.
Not lasers or tasers, not tweezers but Teezers
Investment possibilities. Get your own franchise!

CALL ANYTIME.
That's 999-ANY-TIME.

MINUTES AND YEARS
Michael Miller

The electronic lady on
my phone card
tells me that my minutes
are almost gone.
So, with a few key strokes and
my credit card number
I buy enough minutes to last
until summer.

I wondered if somewhere
at the gas station
or the drug store
there might be a card for buying
additional years.
If life is good and
friendships full
I could perhaps buy
ten or fifteen more.
But if health fails and
loved ones go
I might just
not renew.

I know the electronic lady
would understand.

CHARACTERS

BOW-LEGGED
Gary Melom

He was just a bow-legged
old guy
all denim and moustache
and hat
little bitty boots
and big hands.

He looked like he'd spent
his formative years
in the saddle.

But it was just
rickets in Minneapolis
and him playing the cards
he was dealt
and going out to Laramie
once a year
for stories.

NEIGHBORS
Shannon King

On the way to writing poems,
I was distracted by my neighbors.

She -- by the curb, bent and pulling
seat covers on her 1950 jeep.
"I was up all night making these." she said.

He -- stopping to admire, opens his jacket.
He is wearing a car seat belt around his waist.
"I got this at Lava Lounge," he said.
"I had to buy it -- it has my initials. See 'GM'"

Me -- I only have my beat-up Dodge;
no passion for car or self that keeps me up all night
or makes me lay out cash for my initials; but I feel blessed.
I have neighbors who set examples –
who keep my imagination on its toes.

RELATIVES
Anita Ross

My sister travels on a grasshopper
wears nails around her ankles
wraps rainbows in mud.

My father walks sideways in the sand
opens rocks with his eyes
flows like blood through my tears.

My mother sleeps under a leaf
slides through the light
rides words across the table.

And I sing artichokes into bloom
paint yellow and purple sonatas
write teapots into poems.

AQUAMAN
Rebecca Surmont

We were in "Contemporary American Writers".
He hovered silently as a fish in the back of the room.
How appropriate we were reading Moby Dick;
The drones of nautical notation,
anti-climactic waves of adjectives
And a character, obsessive, unrelenting
To snare his beast.
"Call me Ishmael."

We called the mysterious guy in the back, "Aquaman."
It was his blue polyester suit
Worn a little too tightly - an aerodynamic body filling it -
and barrel chest I was sure housed molded 6-pack abs which
Promised buoyancy and longevity for swimming
Miles under the weight of water.
Out of a contrasting coral-red turtleneck,
Sprouted an oval head with slick brown hair and a
Completely non-expressive face, wide enough for
where the gills should have been.
His suit was second-hand proof his needs were few.
That was all he ever wore.

The full moon delivered an isolated aura
That hanged breathless as I
Entertained death in a depressive march to class.
I thought how often I felt the keel of my
thoughts steering away and toward
The center of expiration so quickly.
My ocean drying up, bones adrift,
My soul released like fish.
English Departments couldn't breed that
Much unhappiness, could they?
I answered, "No" that day - and every day after.
My victory. I walked.

We were curious he hadn't shown up for the
Lectures for two classes.
Where was Aquaman
in his swampy-smelling, sea–blue suit?
We got the word that speared us all --
He too had dwelt in isolation,
compelled to fell a beast beyond the deep,
a wailing demon so formidable: himself.

He didn't know his own power.
It only took one try --
One rope, one stool, one step
One month before graduation. No net.
I wondered if he had worn the red turtle neck.
I imagined him swimming eternally and
I hated Moby Dick.

THE QUEEN
Victoria Raphael

The Queen sits by the window in her pajamas
regally eating shredded wheat
with the silver spoon that came from the drawer
instead of her mouth.

She views her kingdom from an upper window,
counting the minutes until she must descend
to street level and hold court on a crowded bus.

Until then she will do the things
that no longer matter to most people:
color coordinate her ensemble,
match purse and shoes,
then apply lips and eyes
before going out amongst her public.
The ear plugs beneath her hair
will make it easy to tune them out
when they use unintelligible slang, poor grammar,
or obscenities within earshot.

The wind is blowing.
"I guess I shall leave my tiara at home today," says she,
telling the Cat to guard it well
as she will wear it later when she watches the telly.
She then departs for her office --
no longer a queen, but a corporate drone in disguise.

In the evening she returns to her high rise palace,
then changes into a silken dressing gown
and a pair of Chinese slippers
before sipping a glass of port.
Eager to unruffled her peacock feathers
she turns up the symphony,
feeds the Cat from a crystal goblet,
then presents leftovers to herself on a Wedgewood plate.

At midnight the Queen retires to her chambers,
takes a bubble bath,
then covers her eyes with a satin sleep mask.
She dreams of imaginary places
where there are no busses, cell phones, nor Ipods…
a world where men shave and tuck in their shirts,
children are polite, and cubicles are closets
and not places where people work,
where doing one thing at a time is still good,
and no one uses the words   "cool" or "awesome"
unless they are referring to sherbet
or a range of mountains.

THE FIELDS SLIPPED BY
Anita Ross

The fields slipped by
all muted browns and greys,
ragged with cornstalks,
stitched together by lines
of black earth and dirty snow.
A timid sun peeked cautiously
through colorless clouds,
then hid from the whining wind.

If I squint, the browns and greys
blur and become moire silk.
My grandmother had a dress like that.
It whispered when she walked.

She was beautiful,
all muted browns and greys,
ragged with time,
stitched together with threads
of other peoples lives.
A quiet woman saying little,
letting grandpa do the talking,
going about her own business.

My mind squints, her features
blur and become mine.
All I need is a silk dress
that whispers when I walk.

THE STOP SIGN AND THE TAGGER'S INTENT
David Banks

he might have been out of ammunition
or, lacking the aim or violent ambition,
could not shoot holes in its theory.

yet clearly he took offense
to its red-faced dogma —
to its no-two-ways-about-it demand.

how he must have hated it:
rigid yet reflective in the night.

so he approached it with his mushroom mark,
spraying his flourish far past
the clean edge of authority,

immune to the head-turning plea
repeated in perpetuity
as time and time's accomplices roll by.

RELATIVE
Kevin Zepper

The honey brown marmoset
at the Wakeville Zoological Gardens
continues to scratch his privates
in front of me
through the glass divider of the cage.
I find something familiar
in the pink naked face
staring back at me through the glass,
tropical boughs criss-crossing
the marmoset jungle cubicle.

Uncle Jake, it's Uncle Jake.
That's him, he always does that
at family gatherings.
He doesn't care if I see him
scratching his testicles or not,
grilling steaks, burning weenies,
drinking beer and accidentally
puncturing people with lawn Jarts.
When he drank,
he called everyone "bananas"
and tried to tug his trousers up
to mask his vertical smile.

I look closer in the cage and realize
this marmoset has no pencil-thin mustache.
That's Jake's trademark,
his shadow of masculinity.
I mistook the marmoset for someone else,
another relative perhaps.
I scratch my butt and wonder who.

CASH REGISTER BLUES
David Banks

certainly there's pain.
the gene pool didn't just do that
to the woman at the counter.
no one's frown can stretch like that,
around the head, attached in back,
without the tug of torment.

so i ask her how she is, and she says
fine, don't worry
[that my daughter's molten lava,
my mother's turned to stone,
and I'm the smothered mantle
in between].
then she counts my change precisely,
pinching coins so tightly
that they might release compassion
were they not restrained as metals,
and flings them at my hand
without encroaching on the space
within which pity —
germs may transmit.

JOB BOARD SONG
Rebecca Surmont

Oh, I'm a Six Sigma Black Belt (handy with karate chops)
Human Resource Strategist – Marketing-Account-Exec
Programmer and Brand Expert-Engineer-Receptionist-
Data Entry Architect
Lab technician, what the heck!
Point of purchase, biz to biz, I don't care what job it is,
I'll be your anything.

They say you need more training
And then you've got too much.
Your Face Book isn't up to date
And you're not linked enough.
Computer skills are slacking,
Experience is lacking
You're six months into your new job
And then they send you packing!
I'll be your anything.

Tracking and analysis (guarantee for paralysis)
Implement and ideate (sounds too good to hesitate)
Design! Direct! Create! Consult!
Survey says: "Generate, Gestalt!"

They tell me I need to learn about social media
But I'm beginning to feel like an encyclopedia!
I admit I feel a Twitter and all tubed up,
My mind is racing like it's been lubed up.
No conversation necessary –
I'm just a click away –
You can view my profiles any time of day.
My network is extensive - from here to Mexico -
Feel free to check my website for what you want to know.
Or ask a friend on Face Book - though they don't know me well
But at least we're friends forever
And there's nothing they won't tell!
I am Innovation!
I am Transformation!
There's just one caveat
Regarding my situation -
I have no transportation.

But I'll be your anything!!!

HOOD
Kevin Zepper

Yes, she did save her grandmother,
but what happened after
was quite a different story.

It was Red Riding Hood, not the woodsman,
who killed the cross-dressing wolf.
As the woodsman paused,
Miss Hood took the grand axe
and pummeled the wolf into furry pulp.

Surprised, the woodsman
scolded the young girl.
A fatal swipe with the ax
was Riding Hood's response.
Her grandmother says nothing
about either incident.
In fact, she rarely says anything
these days about Miss Hood.

Now, the red-hooded girl is known
as Red-Righting Hood, Storybook Vigilante.
Her smile forever shaped like a wary brow,
she waits at the edge of the wood -- waits –
with her hatchet nestled in her basket.

LIFE, LIVING AND TRANSITIONS

REGRESSION PROGRESS
G. Scott

If you could live your life backwards,
And find yourself younger each day,
You'd start out dead, then rise from the grave,
And get the worst part out of the way.

You'd wake up in a home or a hospice,
Feeling better as each year goes by.
You'd get kicked out for being too healthy,
While the staff remarked you're too spry.

You'd go to collect on your pension
And live on retirement pay.
And when you got young enough to work,
You'd get your gold watch the first day.

You'd work 40 years, till the job got old,
But you were still in your prime.
You'd drop out of the work force, and go to school
To booze and have a good time.

You'd take all of your classes without any cares;
And with no need to study—just play.
You'd have no concerns about getting good grades:
See, you got your diploma first day.

Then you'd play in the sandbox with all of your toys,
And not have a care on this earth.
You'd go back to the breast, and your mother's arms,
Up until the day of your birth.

You'd return to the womb, getting smaller,
And be reduced to mere protoplasm;
Then become an egg in a fallopian tube,
And finish off as a hearty orgasm.

SPEED
Michael John Kennedy

Don't answer your cell phone.
Put away your watch.

Turn off the air conditioner.
Open the windows and
let your hair get messy.

Smell the fields and
the breakfasts.
Listen to the motorcycles
and tires on the road.

Now turn off the interstate
get on a two-lane road
and for god's sake slow down.
You wanted a car trip
now here it is.

Don't calculate how many miles
you have to go.
Keep an eye out for a good
BLT and hot apple pie.
Count how many deer you see.
Look at an abandoned house and
go on in.

What's your hurry?
This is your trip
your time
your life.
Let it be rich in the little highways
nobody wants to see.

Yes, you have a goal
but nobody said it had to be imminent.
Evil spirits travel on straight lines
Be circuitous.

TALKING ABOUT MY GENERATION
Doug Wilhide

"We are always the same age inside."
-- Gertrude Stein

So how did we suddenly become
distinguished speakers?
graybeard sages from the '60s?
damn near as old as we look?
solid citizens?
estimable personages?

We have buried friends, buried parents,
some of us have buried children.
We have put bread on the table
put up with institutions
changed lovers, jobs, dreams and hair.
We have ridden life's little roller coaster,
hands in the air.

We have traveled widely
experienced cultures and eaten well
drunk too much too often
and had almost enough sex.
We've been stupid, wise, funny, boring
careless and caring.
We have been both selfish and sharing.

We have raised children and dogs (and cats)
and seen them leave us.
We have discussed, debated and worried over
everything from redecorating to Republicans.
We have biked, skated, swum and run and called it fun.

We have survived.
And now, every morning, we must face the mirror
and lie to ourselves --
or, to tell the truth, maybe not.
At this stage in life we must be fair:
Look closer: isn't that you in there?

DANCE YOUR STANCE
Howard Arthur Osborn

You've been walking your talk
putting your money where your mouth is
taking a stand.
You've walked for peace, for a dollar a mile –
for frustration -- and just for the hell of it.

You've had your children walk through fire
Jack be nimble Jack be quick
Jack jump over the candlestick
You've made them jump through hoops
thread the needle - and even
learn to stay within the lines
while walking flat mazes

If the next generation fails
it won't be your fault.

But then—what do you stand for?
and against?
Change?

If the only thing certain is change
there's no way to say
or stay which way it will go?
where it will stop? or when?
—sometimes you fall one way
sometimes the other.

Like dancing
change only stops to catch its breath
to catch the rhythms of the next piece
and for exhaustion
and by then it's too late—so

Dance your stance.
Put joy in this exhausting life
add your own clamor to life's worries and woes
reflect on the best
in your rear-view mirror
things are closer than you think
don't back up to the brink!

relax at country fairs –
watch cows ruminate
pow wows extravagate
get the beat then add your feet
dance lines and squares
integrate   syncopate   improvise!

Old tunes find new rhythms
old limbs   young limbs
squares gays and straights
mold old rhymes into the new.

Yes! dance your stance!
be nimble be quick avoid the candlestick
Just you wait 'enry 'iggins
we'll find Matilda waltzing
in Tennessee
wearing her bling.

Then 'fair lady' don't you fret
we won't forget
we'll get you to the church on time.

CROSSROADS
Michael John Kennedy

Don't say you made a deal with
devils or creatures of the night.
Nobody buys that crap.
The challenge of the crossroad is not in selling souls.
People do that every day.

The romance of all that
is reserved for Robert Johnson.
For the rest of us it's
Chrome-plated bumpers
that don't work at high-speed impact.

The challenge is in diving through
the invisible.
Trusting the air and water.

Keeping your focus
once you realize
the trip is well underway
and the road back
is vapor.

So deal with it.
You made your wish.
You rubbed the lamp
and stepped on the carpet.
Now ride!

A SECOND GLASS OF SANCERRE   (for Deb)
Doug Wilhide

There was no reason the two young people
began dancing there beside the road
no reason to their well-executed twists and turns;
a radio on their motorcycle was playing music --
samba -- and so they danced.

A friend of mine hid happily behind her sunglasses
at a back table in front of the Deux Maggots
watching the tourists and the traffic pass by.
She had ordered a second glass of white wine
and it sat there, comforting, catching the sunlight.

She felt fine. She was dying. She knew this.
The docs had said it had spread and outlined her options.
She turned them down and went to Paris
to see the art, to walk around the city once more.
She had -- weeks? months? Maybe into September?
She felt fine now, and had time to sip sancerre at her leisure

The young man and the young woman twisted
hips arms torsos together -- a fine rhythm overtaking them
Samba! They danced before the afternoon sunlight,
shadows held up against the future.

DEMENTIA
David Banks

Call it what you want, this thigh-high slurry,
misty-eyed, whirring reality of mine.
In darker moments, I know what I am.

Company comes again. The soup broth is thin.
What's that you whisper? Secrets or sins?
That man — that woman — they barge right in
like they own the place. Red jack,
black ten reveals the ace. Why,
they take what they want and slap
my face and leave me alone.
They won't take me home.
I want to go home!

Withering woman ... automatic mind ...
I hear you talking.
Forget what I know. Find me my love,
who was lost and was here just moments ago.

ELSIE
Cathy Cato

Whenever she dreamed,
she was able to either wake up
or choose the happy ending,
then – she became ill.

she still had the voice
she used on the phone
or for company: only
those closest to her
heard a slight change... less
loud with a lower timbre.
Talk of miracles began
to fade, but her voice
would not say "cancer."

Saying something out loud makes it true.

One afternoon in the privacy
of her room, with the shades
closed to the Arizona sun,
we laid on our backs
and viewed the ceiling. She said,
"Sometimes, if I lie still
in this position just right,
it doesn't hurt. I can almost
forget." She took my hand

and continued to look straight
at the ceiling. I took on
the same position, knees
pointed skyward – one hand
firmly holding her hand,
helping her...
as if she were crossing a street
for the first time.

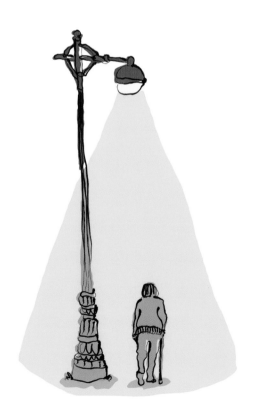

TRAGEDIES
Scott Devens

i read about how
some of the men felt
who were involved
in that bridge disaster

of how
the worst thing for them
would have been
never seeing their families
again

tragedies
whole lives, whole dreams
falling out from under us
really big, important things
falling apart
treasured pictures
instantly gone

the accident, or the news
then the sudden shift

weightlessness
scared to hit bottom
grasping at anything
holding to hope

falling down
thinking of loved ones
praying for safety

the past
flashing before our eyes
the future
not what was expected.

WHAT DREAMS MAY COME
Doug Wilhide

My brother-in-law died in his sleep
a couple years ago.
He was on a trip with a friend,
went to sleep and didn't wake up.
Heart attack.
Massive myocardial infarction, as the docs say.
Probably didn't feel a thing.
Arms behind his head in the same position
as when he said good night.
My age.

My sister, never one of the calmest of souls,
was shipwrecked.
She heaved great tsunamis of grief on the world
and after a year was still breaking down
in great waves that now have become
regular, steady rollers --
the background noise of her
life on the beach.

I have noticed twinges recently:
a little pain in the chest now and then,
an unexpected shortness of breath
if I climb too far too fast on hiking trails
or tackle a few flights of stairs.
It comes and goes away
and I'm inclined to ignore it.

But every night I pray,
and as I lay me down to sleep
listen to my heartbeat say:
not yet
not yet
not yet.

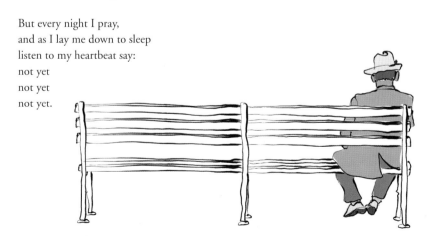

The Poets

Joe Alfano is a science specialist with the Minneapolis Public Schools. He also is a father, a husband and a part-time musician who can play Edelweiss on the musical saw. He has been walking around (and, in winter, across) Lake Harriet for decades.

Cristopher Anderson is a writer, documentary film maker, musician and teacher who contributes to his wife's (Maria Genné) Kairos Dance Theater program for elders. He has been a book store clerk, bartender and seaman in the Danish Merchant Marine.

David Banks has been a journalist for 20 years and is currently an editor with the Minneapolis *Star Tribune*. He likes taking in the world from the public crossings of coffee shops but also makes a fine home cappuccino.

Karen Barstad is a compliance officer at a Minneapolis bank. She has given a public reading of her collected writings, *The Hope Factor*. She is the granddaughter of the foreman of the jury that found Wilbur Foshay guilty of mail fraud in 1932.

Tanja Birke is a registered nurse and the mother of two artistically inclined children. She also has worked with Waldorf Schools, published five chapbooks of poetry and "really believes in magic."

Chuck Boe left a career in corporate finance to teach Reiki healing and do tarot readings. He lives in the Kingfield neighborhood, near lakes Calhoun and Harriet.

Sandra Burwell has been a teacher of early childhood and primary students. She is a long time resident of southwest Minneapolis and married to a "serious and funny man from North Dakota."

Phil Calvit is an advertising creative director and life-long southwest area resident. By and large he prefers Lake Harriet over Lake Calhoun. He enjoys writing poetry because only he has to approve it.

Maria Campo writes poetry in English and Italian and has published a book of poetry, *Love, Lust and Loss* (2009). She likes reading, cooking, gardening and traveling.

Cathy Cato is a registered nurse and an executive with a disability management firm. On the night the Edmund Fitzgerald sank, she climbed up the icy steps to the operator's house on the Duluth lift bridge.

Scott Devens is an elementary teacher and a writer in Linden Hills. He is working on an upbeat children's book about friendship to be dedicated to his son Spencer.

Christine Fraser is raising two young children. She has worked as an editor with McGraw-Hill, is (slowly) writing a novel and once worked as a sailor on a replica of Francis Drake's Golden Hind.

Robert Guard is the creative director of Seed Strategy, a marketing services firm outside Cincinnati. He has attended the *Kenyon Review* writer's workshops and had poems published in several journals.

D.B. Hart is a technical writer and quality manager at a Bloomington testing lab. She also has worked as an oncology nurse, tour guide and hanger sorter and once bought Elvis Costello a beer in a bar in New York.

Dave Hutchinson is a sign language interpreter. He also has worked as a driving instructor, janitor and bartender. He makes leather accessories, plays guitar and frequently wears a bow tie.

Michael John Kennedy teaches English at Southwest High School. He writes poetry, short fiction and essays and has been an actor and photographer. He has written a book, *The Off-the-Record Handbook for Teaching High School English.*

Shannon King taught college literature classes for 15 years. She attended the Iowa Writer's Workshop and has published poems in several books and journals. She also has sold popcorn at the Suburban World theater and produced a film for Gedney's pickles.

Amber Lampron works in special education with the Richfield public schools. She moved to Minneapolis from Maine, one of twelve moves throughout her life. She currently lives in Linden Hills but "aches" for a country home with room to roam.

Owen Lazur is a high school student who moved to Minneapolis from New Jersey. He has walked in the canopy of the Peruvian rain forest and describes most of his writing as "schoolwork."

Diana Lundell has written two collections of poetry and is working on her third. She has aspirations of owning a motorcycle and reading 144 books in a year.

Deb Malmo is a corporate communication manager who has written for CEOs and done a wide variety of freelance projects. She is an excellent whistler and can keep a hula hoop going "forever."

Gary Melom is a Hennepin County social worker. He also is a photographer and an accomplished oral storyteller.

Michael Miller is a retired real estate agent. He also has served in the Peace Corps, worked on social policy research, sung with the Dale Warland singers and once swam the Mississippi at the U of M on a dare. He has a lake cabin and eleven grandchildren.

Karyn Milos is a writer and editor who also works as a retail customer service manager. She has written dozens of short stories, poems and satires, and is working on a novel about a same-sex marriage in 1920s and '30s America.

Gayle Mohrbacker retired from the Canadian consulate in Minneapolis and recently moved to Oakland to be near her children (not to escape winter). She lives in a sunny apartment near a fragrant sequoia tree.

Sandra Nelson is an advertising and marketing consultant. She is an ex-Navy brat who can't swim and attended thirteen schools in her first twelve years. She has recently bicycled in France, Italy and South Africa.

Howard Arthur Osborn is a retired agricultural economist who grew up in Saskatchewan. He has published several books of poetry, including *Poems for the Ears* (2008). He served three years in the Canadian army without completing basic training.

Carole Maria Ostlund is a corporate travel consultant who has recently taken up singing with a rock band and jazz trio. She has worked as a teenage model, flight attendant and speaks Spanish and English.

Adam Overland is a communications coordinator at the University of Minnesota. In addition to being a writer he also has worked as a pharmacy technician, a pool boy and an airline baggage handler. Some day he would like to travel in space.

Ross Plovnick is a retired industrial research chemist. He holds a Ph.D from Brown University and his poetry has been published in several journals. He enjoys walking Lake Calhoun and visiting Arizona.

Victoria Raphael is a life coach specializing in inter-cultural/diversity coaching. She likes big band music, travel and yoga and sponsors a penguin in Chile. Her cat, Hemingway, was named "pet of the week" by the *Star Tribune*.

Anita Ross is a retired art teacher and active painter who spent summers at a cottage on Lake Minnetonka before moving permanently to Minneapolis from Nebraska. She likes to read and travel and see her seven grandchildren.

Jim Russell is a retired advertising executive with deep roots in the Minneapolis lakes area. Several of his short stories have been published.

George Scott (G. Scott) is a retired ad agency media planner who lived in Linden Hills until a recent move to Bloomington. His recent book of limericks and other poems, *The Adult Garden of Verses,* sold out its print run in area bars.

Ben Shank is a business and technical writing expert who gives writing workshops in the United States, Canada, and England. He's a playwright, licensed psychologist and once was an accomplished magician.

Rebecca Surmont is a management consultant and also works as an actor. She is originally from Michigan, has two masters degrees and two dogs, and was a professional mime who studied with Marcel Marceau.

Jacquie Trudeau is a family counselor who has taken courses at the Loft and is part of a writing group. She once won a vacation to Mexico from the *StarTribune's* Love Lines contest. She has eight grandchildren.

Barbara Tuttle is a reference librarian. She has published articles and essays in a variety of periodicals and once worked as an organizer for the United Farm Workers in California.

WACSO stands for "Walkin' Around Checkin' Stuff Out." For info and to see more drawings, go to www.GOWACSO.com

Paul Walker is a management consultant who works with robotic systems. He also has loaded trucks for Sears and been a fry cook for Perkins. He volunteers with the Colin Powell Center and participates in triathlons.

Sam Wilhide is a math teacher who is currently teaching English with the JET program in Kobe, Japan. He is a graduate of South High and UW-Madison and an advocate of healthy eating and organic food. He recently learned how to solve a Rubik's cube.

Doug Wilhide is a writer who is the poetry editor for the *Southwest Journal.* He has worked as a copywriter and creative director at several ad agencies (including his own). He is the Poet Laureate of Linden Hills.

Anne Zager works at Trader Joe's. She also is a massage therapist with a certification in Shiatsu, has worked as a nanny, a goat cheese maker and at the Kennedy Center in Washington, D.C., and has run a marathon.

Kevin Zepper teaches at Moorhead State University in the Corrick Center for General Education. He is the author of three chapbooks and his work has appeared on the Slowtrain website.